What Is Equality?

CIVIC VIRTUES

Ava Beasley

CiViCS
FOR THE REAL WORLD™

Rosen Classroom™

Everyone is different.

Everyone is also equal!

Share the markers
with everyone.

Let everyone sit at the table.

Treat everyone the same.

Be nice to everyone.

WORDS TO KNOW

markers

table